Rhymes and blends

Contents

Teachers' notes	1
Rhyming activities	
Listening for rhyme	5-6
Initial letter discrimination	7-8
Word-to-picture rhyme	9-10
Writing rhyming words	11-12
Recognising rhyming words	13-16
Rhyme check sheets	17-18
Blend and digraph activities	
Blend/digraph sheet 1 – st	19
Blend/digraph sheet 2 – fl and th	20
Blend/digraph sheet 3 – ch, sh, tr	21
Blend/digraph sheet 4 – br, pr, fr, dr	22
Blend/digraph sheet 5 – sw, sn, st, sp	23
Crosswords	24-25
Blend/digraph sheet 6 – wh	26
Digraph revision sheet – sh, ch, wh	27
Word search – th	28
Blend/digraph revision sheets	29-32

Teachers' notes

Aims of this book

- To draw attention to rhyme.
- To help children to distinguish between initial letter sounds.
- To provide activities that expect children to listen with attention.
- To draw attention to the letter similarities between rhyming words.
- To draw attention to the need to recognise the single sound of digraphs.
- To encourage children to recognise common blends.
- To encourage children to listen to the small differences between similar blends, for example, 'sm' and 'sn'.

The place and importance of listening to sounds

In order to become confident and competent spellers, children have to be able to link letter sounds with likely spelling patterns. They need to have a clear vision of how a word 'looks', so that they can quickly realise that it 'looks wrong' and then to recognise when the alternatives they try out 'look right'. An essential ingredient in the early stages of becoming a good speller is the ability to recognise rhyme. The studies of Bryant, Bradley and Goswami have shown that children who are able to identify rhyme are more likely to become better spellers and readers (see Bibliography on page 2).

Children are far more likely to be 'picture literate' than 'sound literate' when they come to school. They can already interpret programmes shown on television or video. They are used to seeing the view from a car window race past them as they travel on motorways. However, they seem to pay less attention to sounds. Children need to understand that the sounds they use in speaking can be represented by black marks on a page and that these marks have a logical and fixed sequence, so that, when a word is written using particular letters, it does not become a different word the following week!

Alerting children to the similarity found in rhyme and letting them identify the differences between the rhyming words is the beginning of an understanding of how to represent language in print.

It is very easy for children to misunderstand the instruction given by the teacher. Children are used to identifying the 'odd one out' from a group of objects. Therefore, when asked to identify the word that does not rhyme, they misunderstand the request and try to discover the odd one out – not because it does not rhyme with the other words, but because of its odd subject matter. For example, when given 'hat', 'cat', 'coat' and 'mat', the child will reply that 'cat' is the odd one as she can see a tenuous link between the inanimate objects as opposed to the animal.

Children need a great deal of oral practice to learn what is meant by rhyme and any few moments can be used by the classroom teacher to pose rhyming games and activities. When children can do this from an oral lesson, they are then ready to move towards linking letter shapes to their sounds.

As children develop their reading skills, they also become more aware of the fine phonological differences. They learn to separate the initial letter sound from the rest of the word, to recognise similar 'sounds' within words, to use these when they write, and finally, to map the correct visual pattern on to the word they want to write.

The problem of 'blends'
Children often begin to be able to link an initial letter with its 'simple' sound, and much work is undertaken by teachers and parents to draw a child's attention to this knowledge. However, many children find the move from the 'single-letter' sound to recognising that two consonants written together may constitute a single sound (as in the digraphs th, sh, ch, wh) or a blend (where there are two mouth movements, as in tr, sk or fl) very difficult. They usually begin by isolating the first letter from its partner and then seem unable to link the next letter to this. When writing, they find the combination of the two letters very difficult to identify. Children do need lots of practice in order to become confident with blends. This book aims to support the teacher with this vital activity.

Tracking
Tracking is a useful activity for drawing attention to letter combinations. Tell the children to scan a page of a newspaper or a magazine and to mark the blend when they see it. (Felt-tipped pens are good for this task.) It encourages close attention to the letters and shows the child that blends can be found at the beginning, middle and end of words. It is not intended that the children should try to read the text, rather that they should pay attention to searching for letter combinations.

Bibliography
'Rhyme recognition and reading and spelling in young children' L Bradley in *Pre-A School Prevention of Reading Failure*, R L Masland and M R Masland (eds) (1988) York Press.
Rhyme and Reason in Reading and Spelling, L Bryant and P E Bryant (1985) Ann Arbor University of Michigan Press.
Phonological Skills and Learning to Read: Essays in developmental psychology, G Goswami and P E Bryant (1990) Lawrence Ellbaum Associates.

Notes on individual activities

Pages 5 to 6: Listening for rhyme
Before using these sheets in the classroom, it is essential that both teachers and parents spend time ensuring that the child understands the concept of rhyme and begins to pay attention to the sounds of words. These pictures are not linked to any words on the page so that the child concentrates upon the rhyming link between the pictures and does not rely upon similar letter patterns.

Extension activities
Play lots of rhyming games with the children, in which they either have to produce a rhyming word or identify the rhyme. Ensure that the rhyme is very clear to them, so that they become confident and are prepared to take risks.
- 'Can you solve my riddle?' Tell the children you are thinking of a colour and you are going to give them a rhyming clue, for instance 'I'm thinking of a colour that rhymes with "bed"'; 'I'm thinking of something to wear that rhymes with "lock"'; 'I'm thinking of something to eat that rhymes with "cutter".'
- 'Provide the missing word.' Tell the children you are a poet but you need help to finish your rhyme. Say very simple rhyming couplets, leaving the last word for the children to provide, as in 'We travelled far in daddy's ...'; 'We must eat so I'll cook some ...'; 'I like to run because it's ...'
- Use nursery rhymes and advertisement jingles to alert children to rhyme. Few children today are really knowledgeable about nursery rhymes and parents are often grateful if the school provides a taped version of some of the better-known ones for them to borrow. However, children do seem to be able to pick up some of the rhyming adverts and will happily join in with these!
- Read simple rhymes to the class and encourage the children to join in. Let them try to spot the rhyme. Do use the same rhymes many times, so that the children become familiar with them. If they can join in, they are more likely to consolidate their understanding of the rhyme.

Pages 7 to 8: Initial letter discrimination
These sheets aim to establish how well the child is able to isolate the initial letter sound from the rhyme.

Extension activities
- Ask the children either to tell you, or to draw a rhyming picture to go with, the word that has not been used within each column.
- With adult help, let the children draw a base board for a simple rhyming game. They will need to draw a path going down the page and divide it up into squares. They then select two rhyming pictures from those given on the sheet and stick one on the 'path' of the game and the other around the border. If a player lands on the 'path picture', he has to find the rhyming picture in the border before he can move on.

Page 9 to 10: Word-to-picture rhyme
These sheets enable the child to read simple three-letter words and to then link these with a rhyming picture.

Extension activities
Mount the pictures from the activity on to card. Place the 'cards' face down on the table. Let the children take it in turns to pick up a card and then think of a rhyming word. If they are right, they can keep the card. The winner is the child with the most cards at the end of the game.

Pages 11 to 12: Writing rhyming words
These sheets aim to give the child practice in writing and searching for letter patterns in simple rhyming words. This is the first movement towards helping children to link letter sounds with a letter pattern.

Pages 13 to 16: Recognising rhyming words
These sheets take the child further towards looking at, as well as listening to, rhyme. When children realise that knowing how to write one word can give them access to many others with a similar letter pattern, they become much more confident when writing and reading. It is this realisation that is so important and which provides much support to young readers and writers.

Pages 17 to 18: Rhyme check sheets
These sheets enable the teacher to see how well the child has managed to link letter sound to letter pattern. If a child is making many mistakes, then a closer examination of the reasons is necessary. It may be that the child is still uncertain about the concept of rhyme or is unable to hear the sounds within words.

Pages 19 to 23: Blend/digraph sheets
There are over 33 different blends found at the beginning of words and it is impossible to give enough space to practise this adequately. The blends in these activities have been selected because they are more likely than others to come within the reading and writing experience of young children. For example, 'ph' has not been introduced in this book as most children do not need this letter combination until later.

Children need to be encouraged to make the sound of the blend while completing the activity. In an ideal situation the child would be muttering the blend as she searched for the letters which represent it. For this reason, mazes and tracking exercises are included as they encourage the child to scan the sheets and vocalise the blend.

Pages 24 to 25: Crosswords
These sheets combine blend recognition with the interpretation of direction. The child has to identify the initial blend, write it below the picture and then transfer this on to the crossword. It is essential that the child understands how crosswords work and is able to follow the directional arrow clue given on the page.

Page 26: Blend/digraph sheet 6
This is a tracking exercise to familiarise the children with the letter pattern 'wh'.

Page 27: Digraph revision sheet
This page gives children a composite picture in which to search for words beginning with the digraphs 'sh', 'ch' and 'wh'. One of the most difficult things children have to master is the notion that two letters make only one sound and this page will encourage this particular skill.

Page 28: Word search
This page draws attention to the high-frequency digraph 'th' which occurs in so many important words that cannot be illustrated. Children constantly need to both read and write these words.

Pages 29 to 32: Blend/digraph revision sheets
These four sheets are provided to enable the teacher to check if the child can distinguish between blends and identify the necessary blend at the start of words. Some close letter sounds have been deliberately placed beneath the pictures, for example, 'ch' and 'tr', so that the teacher can assess how well the child can distinguish between them.

Extension games
Many children need a great deal of practice with blends and digraphs and a very effective way of providing this is through playing card games. The photocopiable pictures in this book are a useful resource for making these games. Use plain playing cards, visiting cards or cut cards from thin card. Stick the selected picture on to the middle of the card.

You could use pictures of the following: bridge, bread, brush; pram, prince, present; snowman, snake, snail; tree, trumpet, train; ship, sheep, shark; crab, crown, crocodile; star, stamp, steps; spanner, spoon, spider.

With any card game for young children, it is essential that they have plenty of opportunity for success. Therefore, with each game, it is better to have two cards with the same picture rather than many different blend pictures.

Blend snap (2 players)
Make 24 cards from four selected blends, making two cards for each chosen picture.

How to play: Shuffle the cards and deal them out between two players. Each player takes it in turn to turn over a card from the top of his/her pile. If the pictures start with the same blend or are an identical match, the first player to say 'snap' may pick up the pile of cards on the table. The winner is either the child with all the cards or the one with the most cards by the end of a designated time.

Memory game (2 to 3 players)

How to play: Select up to 24 blend pairs of cards. Place the cards face down on the table. Each player takes it in turn to turn over two cards. If they start with the same blend, the player keeps the cards and has a second turn. If they do not start with the same blend, the cards are turned back and play moves to the next child. The winner is the player with the most sets of pairs at the end of the game.

Pass the digraph (3 to 4 players)

How to play: The object of the game is to collect pairs of blend cards. Make 24 blend pair cards and one digraph card. Deal out all the cards to the players. Players then check if they have any blend pairs. They may put these down on the table. Players then select two cards to pass on to the player on their left. Players then collect two cards from the player on their right. If these cards make any pairs they may place these down on the table. Play then continues until a player is 'out' by putting all the cards down in pairs. The player with the digraph has to give any pairs of cards she has collected to the winner.

NB Many words that start with a blend or digraph cannot be illustrated and therefore teachers do need to draw attention to them. Placing a large sheet of ruled paper on a wall near the door and asking children to write down any specified blend as they notice it during their reading can be very effective. The children will talk about the words and read them to each other while waiting to leave the room. This drawing of attention to the blend or digraph will help less confident readers and writers.

Blend/digraph Ladders

blouse		speed
blow	Which	spend
table	blend will	spill
black	climb the	spider
blue	fastest?	sport
bl		sp

National Curriculum: English

In addition to the PoS for AT1, the following PoS are relevant to this book:

AT2 – Pupils should:
- write some letters in response to speech sounds and letter names. (1b)
- use at least single letters or groups of letters to represent whole words or parts of words. (1c)
- spell correctly in the course of their own writing simple monosyllabic words they use regularly which observe common patterns. (2b)
- recognise that spelling has patterns and begin to apply their knowledge of those patterns to a wider range of words. (2c)

Scottish 5–14 Curriculum: English language

Attainment outcome	Strand	Attainment target	Level
Writing	Spelling	Spelling accurately the words which they need to use most commonly.	A
Reading	Reading for information	Finding an item of information from an informational text.	A

- Name _____

Listening for rhyme – 1

- Colour the pictures in the same line that rhyme.

ESSENTIALS FOR ENGLISH: Rhymes and blends

● Name _____

Listening for rhyme – 2

● Colour the pictures in the same line that rhyme.

ESSENTIALS FOR ENGLISH: Rhymes and blends

- Name _____

Initial letter discrimination – 1

- Colour the two pictures that rhyme.
- Write in the missing letters.

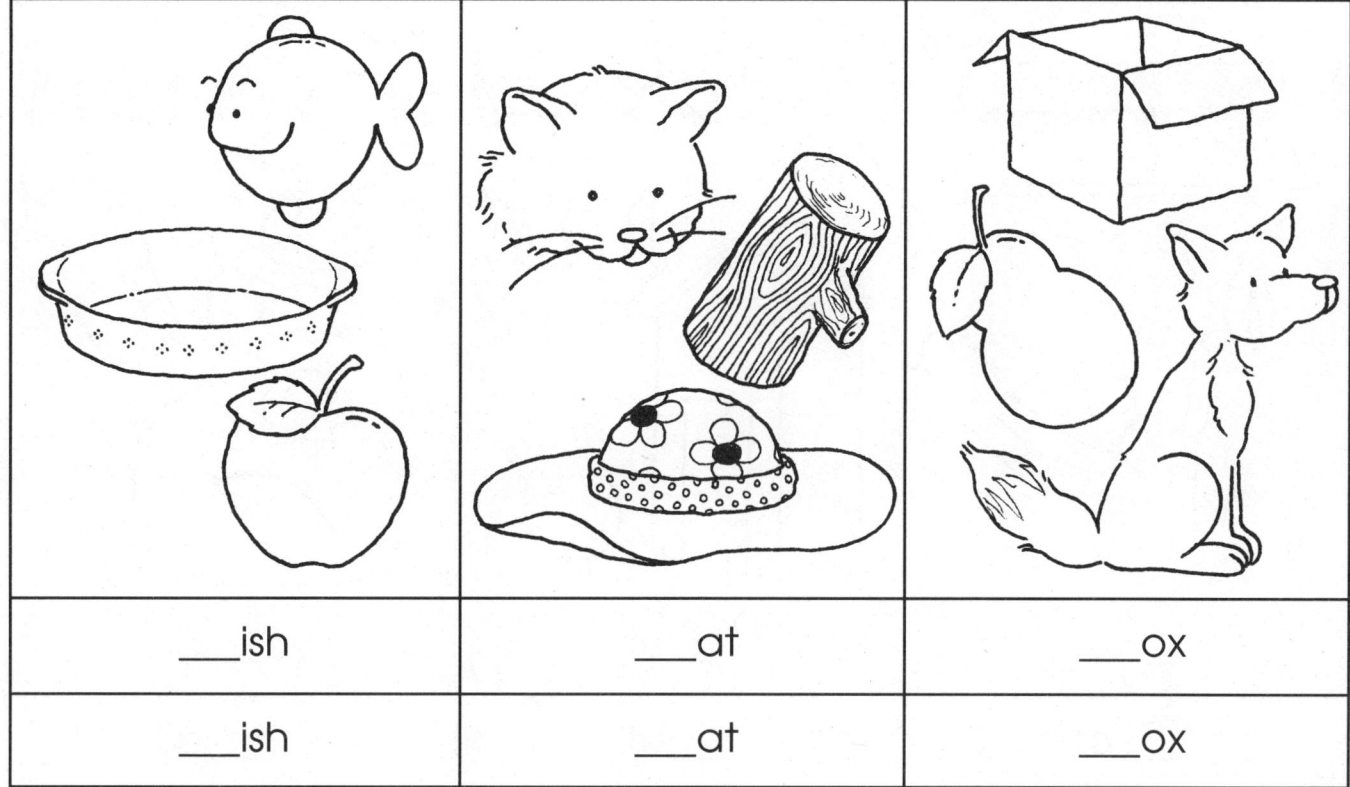

| ___ish | ___at | ___ox |
| ___ish | ___at | ___ox |

| ___an | ___og | ___all |
| ___an | ___og | ___all |

ESSENTIALS FOR ENGLISH: Rhymes and blends

- Name _____

Initial letter discrimination – 2

- Colour the two pictures that rhyme.
- Write in the missing letters.

| __at | __ut | __ig |
| __at | __ut | __ig |

| __oat | __ock | __ook |
| __oat | __ock | __ook |

ESSENTIALS FOR ENGLISH: Rhymes and blends

● Name _____

Word-to-picture rhyme – 1

● Join the words to the rhyming picture.
● Write the name by the picture.

box

fun

red

ten

map

pup

● Name _____

Word-to-picture rhyme – 2

● Join the words to the rhyming picture.
● Write the name by the picture.

ESSENTIALS FOR ENGLISH: Rhymes and blends

Name _____

Writing rhyming words – 1

● Write a rhyming word. Then write the letter pattern. The first one has been done for you.

		Rhyming word	Letter pattern
bad	sad	had	ad
dig	big	_____	_____
run	fun	_____	_____
bed	fed	_____	_____
wet	met	_____	_____
hop	top	_____	_____
mat	sat	_____	_____

ESSENTIALS FOR ENGLISH: Rhymes and blends

- Name _____

Writing rhyming words – 2

● Write a rhyming word. Then write the letter pattern.
The first one has been done for you.

		Rhyming word	Letter pattern
well	bell	tell	ell
sand	hand		
cook	look		
felt	melt		
mend	lend		
fish	wish		
king	sing		

- Name _____

Recognising rhyming words – 1

- Colour red the words that rhyme with **make**.
- Colour yellow the words that rhyme with **link**.

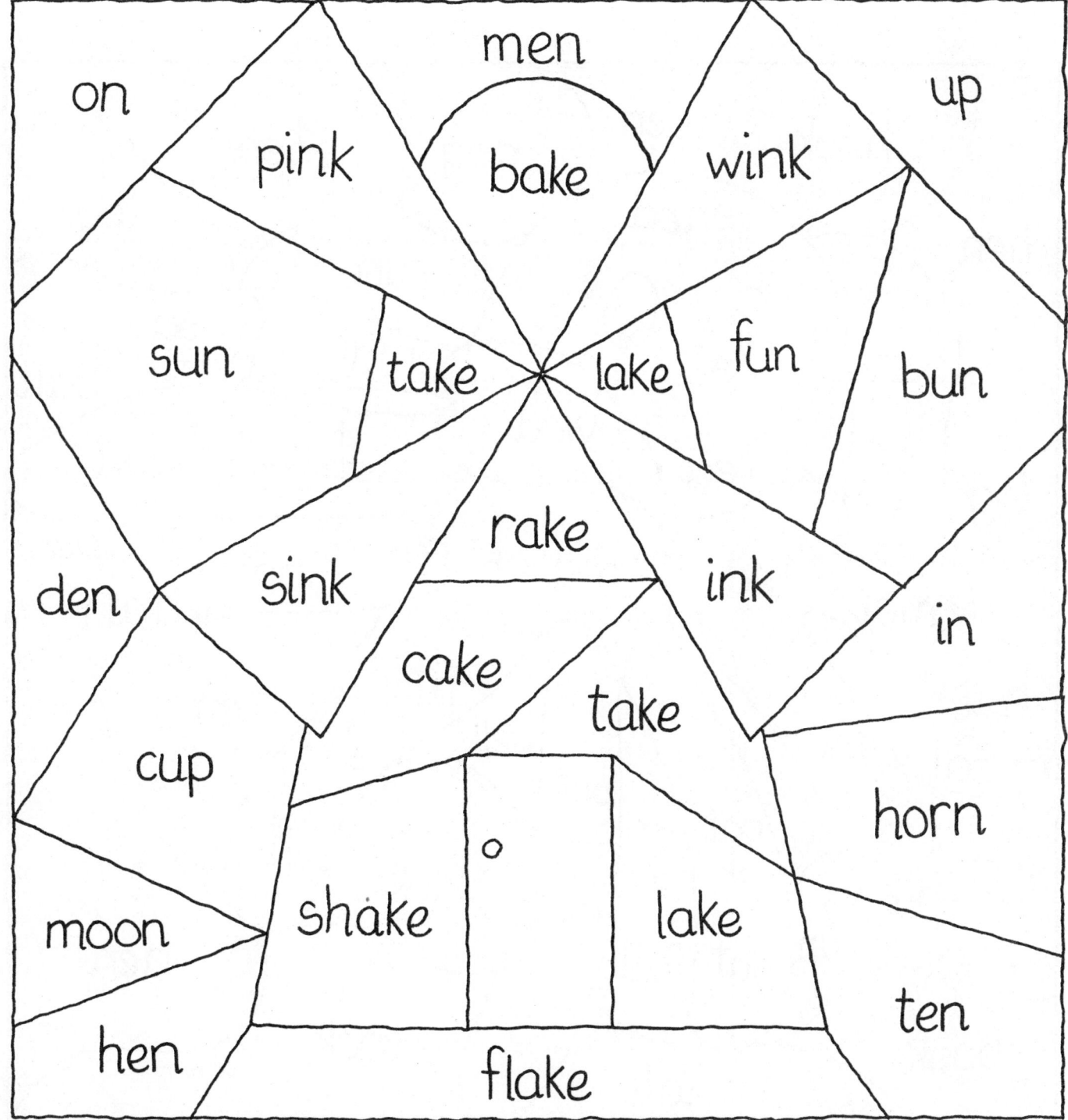

- What have you found? _____

- Name _____

Recognising rhyming words – 2

- Colour blue the words that rhyme with **bed**.

- Colour red the words that rhyme with **bat**.

- Colour green the words that rhyme with **pit**.

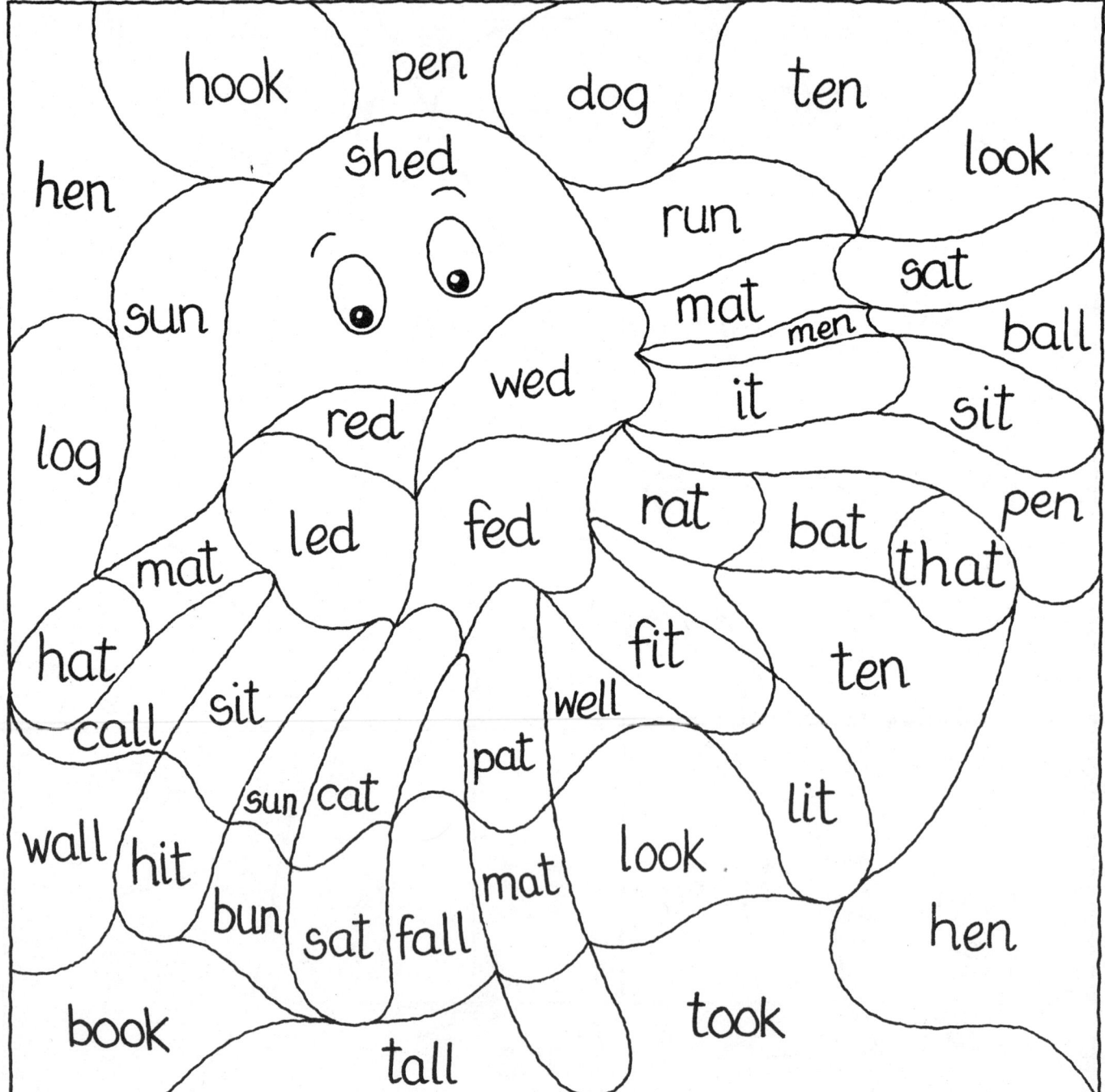

- What have you found? _____

- Name _____

Recognising rhyming words – 3

- Can you reach the gold by finding the rhyming path?

- Now use some of your rhyming words to put in these sentences.

Jack _____ the cow for five beans.

When they opened the sack it was full of _____ .

- Name _____

Recognising rhyming words – 4

- Can you find your way through the fields and over the stiles by finding all the words that rhyme with **end**?

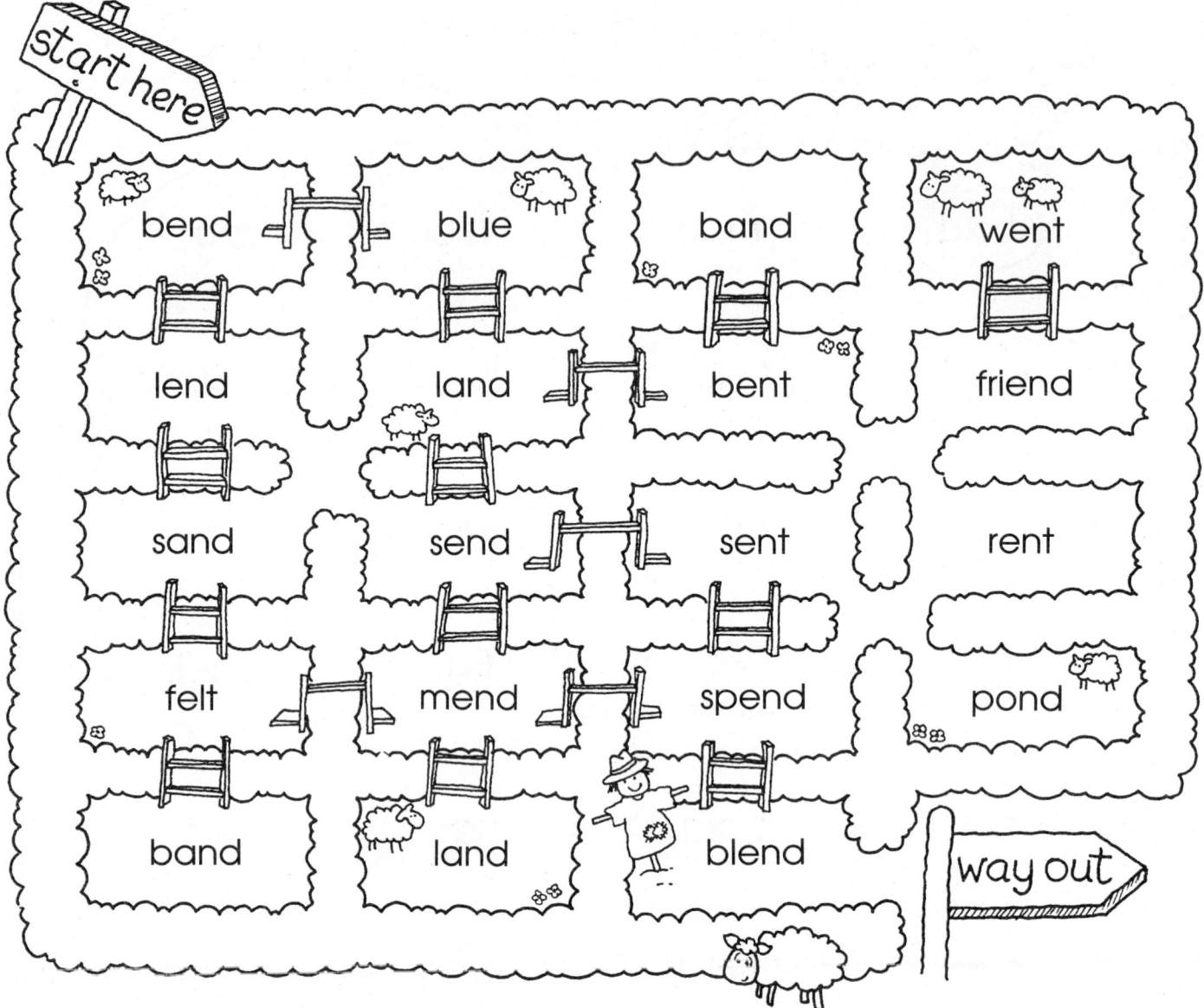

- Now write the words you found on your path.

_____ _____

_____ _____

_____ _____

ESSENTIALS FOR ENGLISH: Rhymes and blends

- Name _____

Rhyme check sheet – 1

- Can you write some words that rhyme?

at	get	not

red	hug	fun

● Name _____

Rhyme check sheet – 2

● Can you write some words that rhyme?

all	old	hook
(wall)	(gold)	(cook)

and	tell	cake
(hand)	(well)	(rake)

- Name _____

Blend/digraph sheet 1 – st

- To reach Earth, you must follow the **st** path.

Name _____

Blend/digraph sheet 2 – fl and th

● Look at these pictures. Listen to the starting sound.

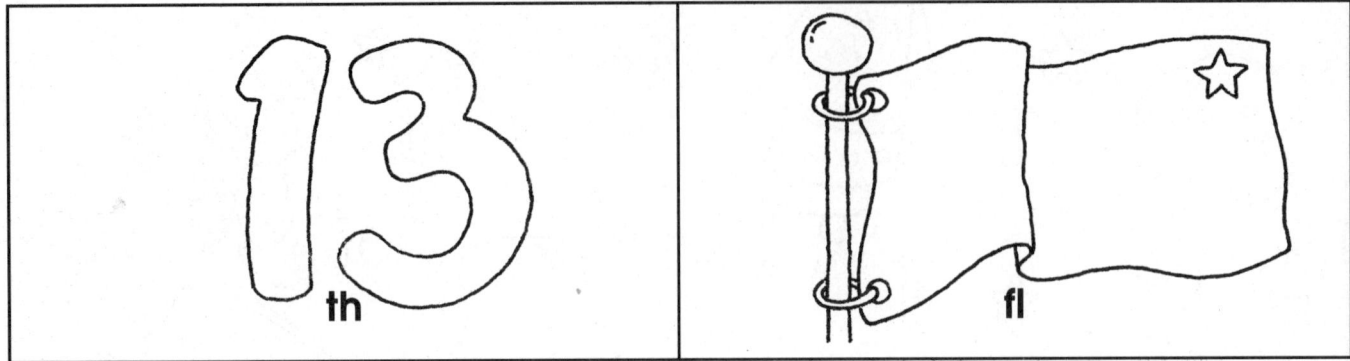

● Write the missing letters to make the words.

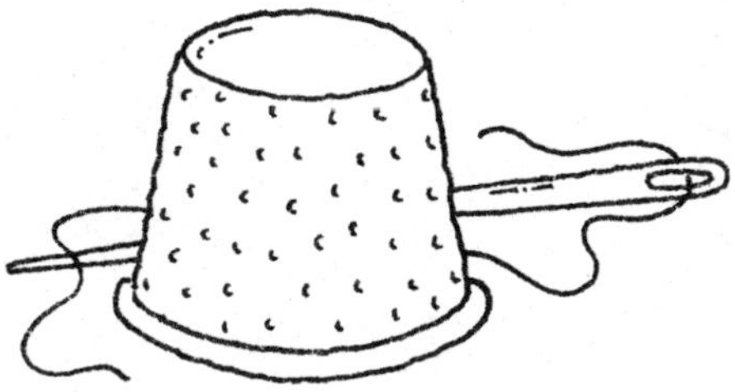

___imble

3 ___ree

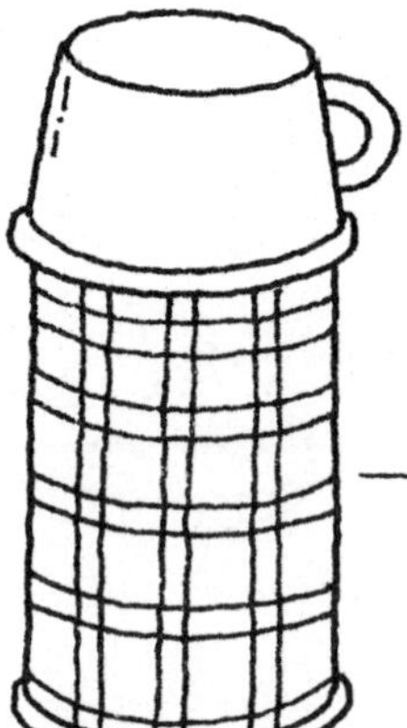

___ask

___y

___ower

___orns

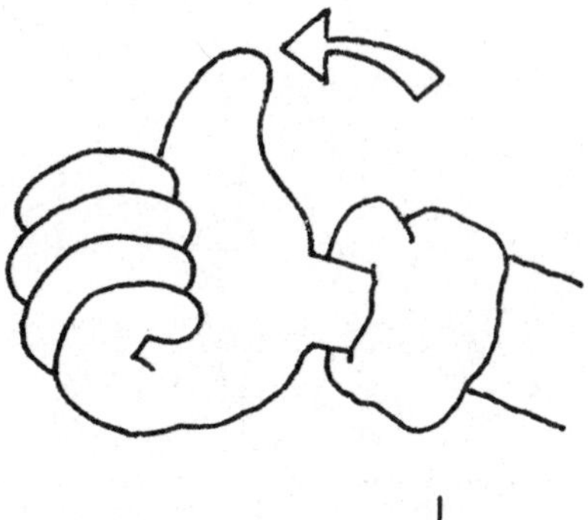

___umb

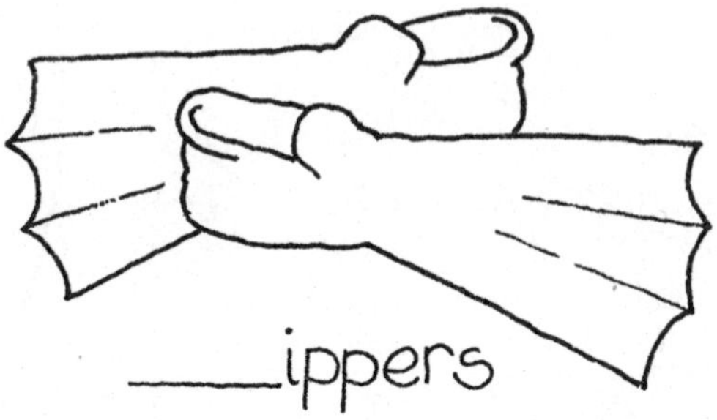

___ippers

ESSENTIALS FOR ENGLISH: Rhymes and blends

Name ______________________

Blend/digraph sheet 3 – ch, sh and tr

- Look at these three pictures. Listen to the starting sound.

ch

sh

tr

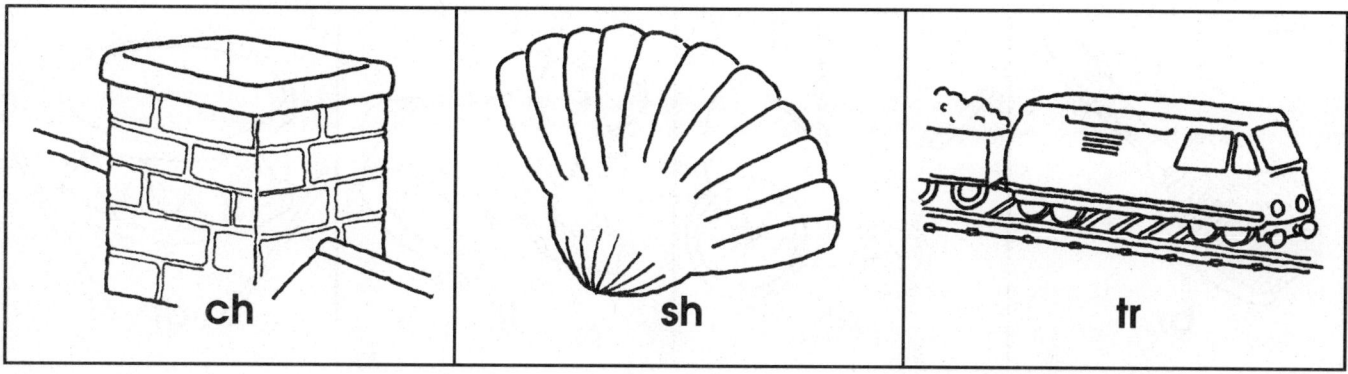

- Can you write the missing letters to make the words?

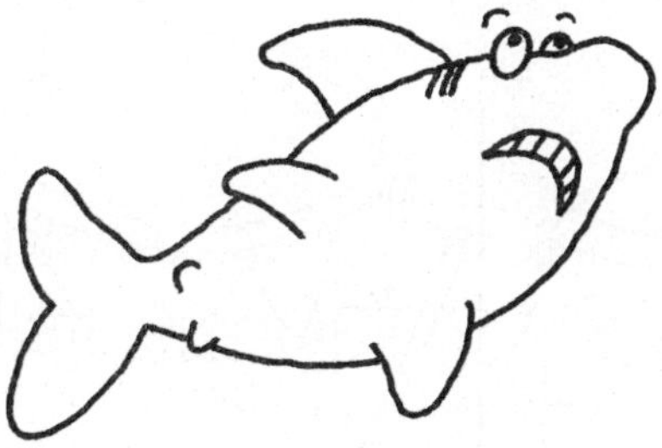

____ark

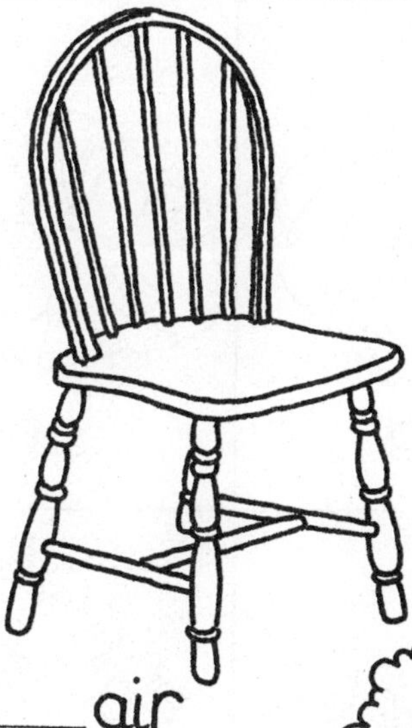

____air

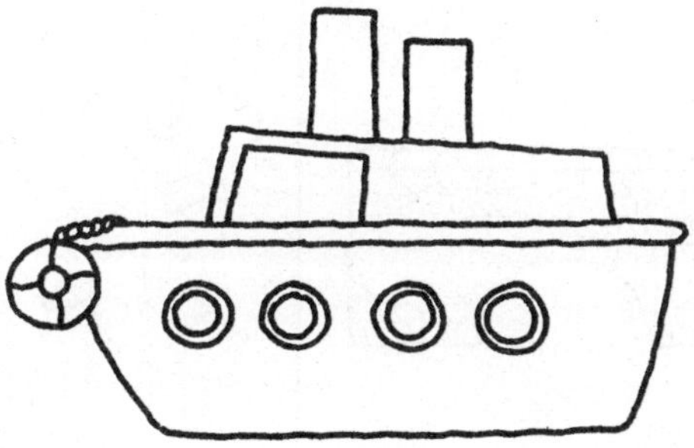

____ip

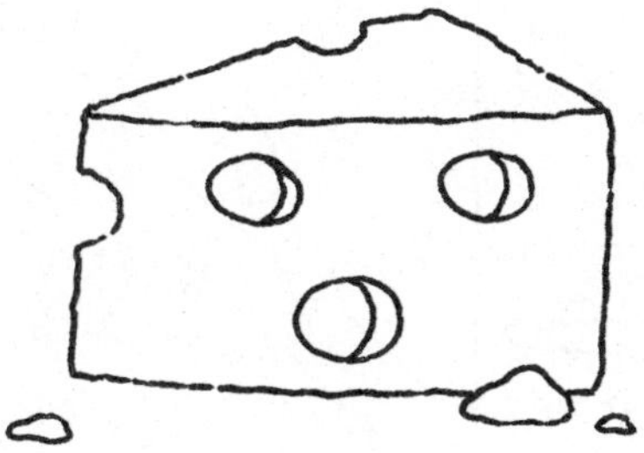

____eese

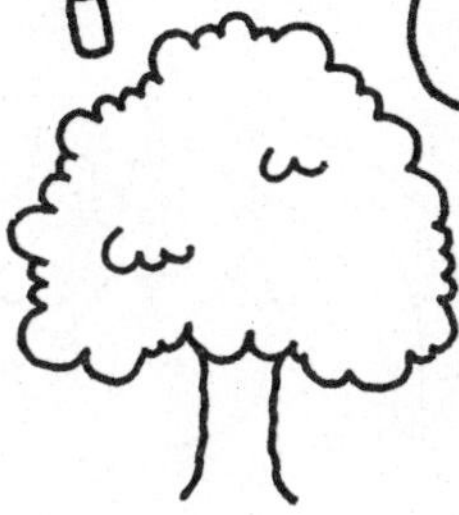

____ee

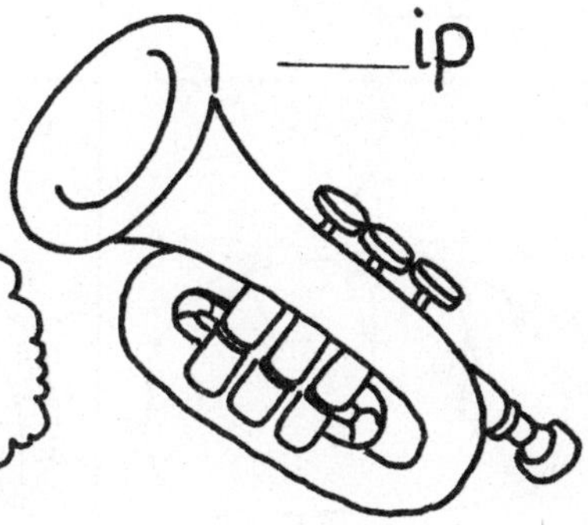

____umpet

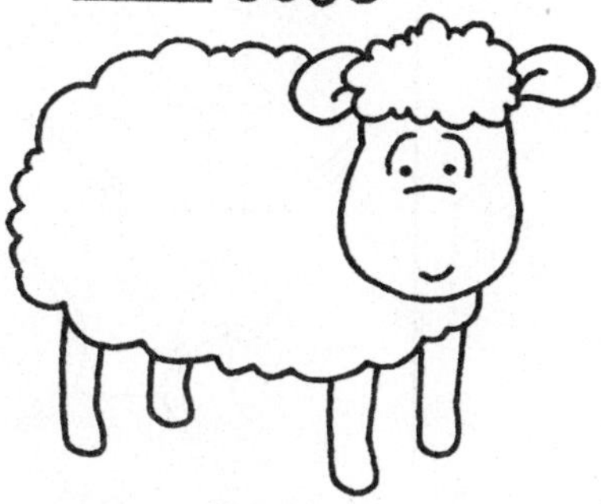

____eep

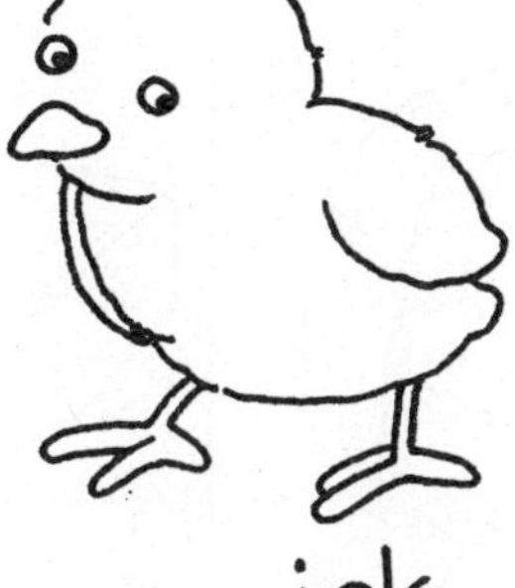

____ick

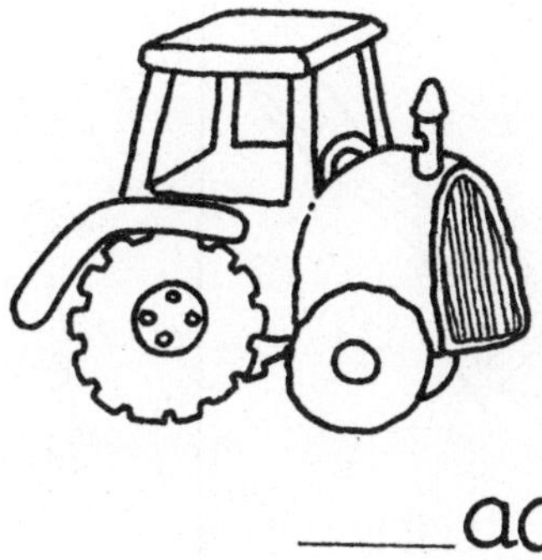

____actor

● Name _____

Blend/digraph sheet 4 – br, pr, fr and dr

● Look at these pictures. Say the starting sounds.

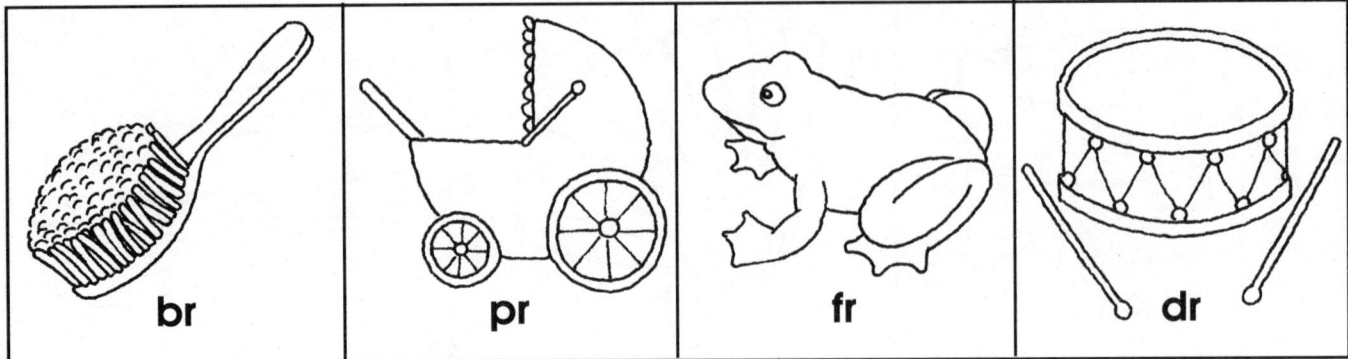

● Write the missing letters to make the words.

 __idge	 __og	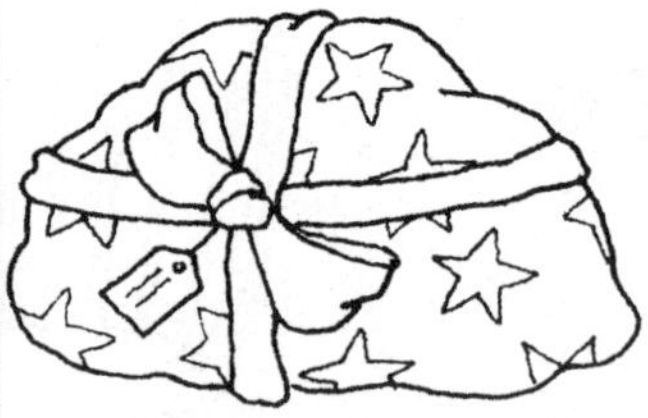 __esent	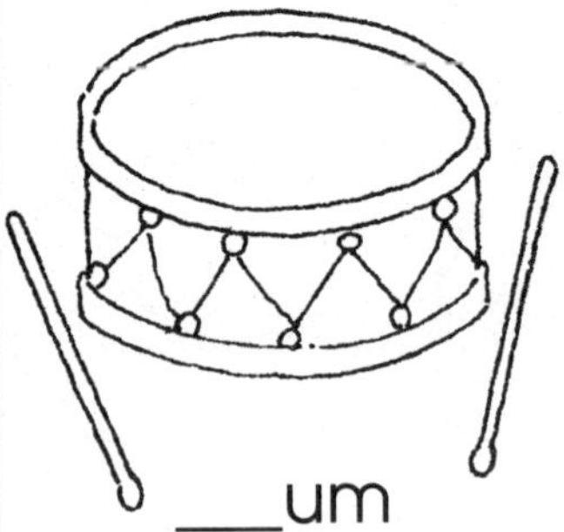 __um
 __ead	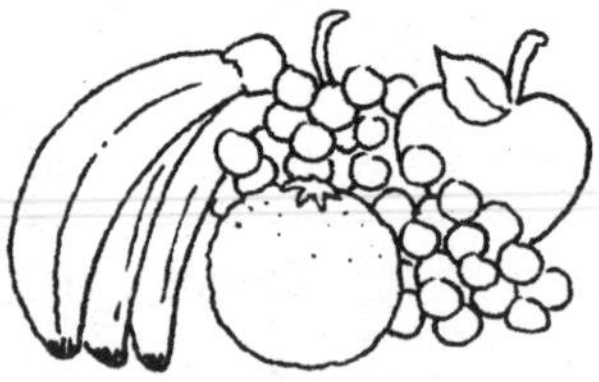 __uit	 __agon	 __anch
 __ush	 __ess	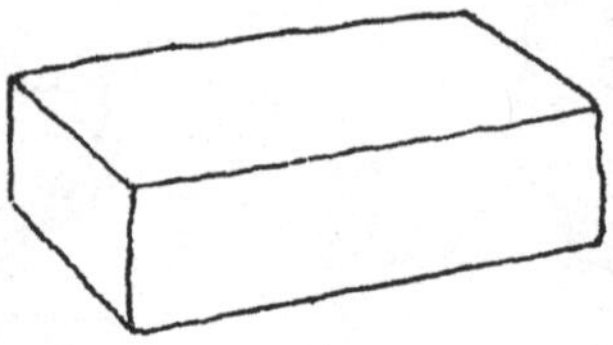 __ick	 __am

ESSENTIALS FOR ENGLISH: Rhymes and blends

- Name _____

Blend/digraph sheet 5 – sw, sn, st and sp

- Colour the pictures that start with the same sound.

ESSENTIALS FOR ENGLISH: Rhymes and blends

• Name _____

Crosswords – 1

• Write in the missing letters, then fill in the crosswords.

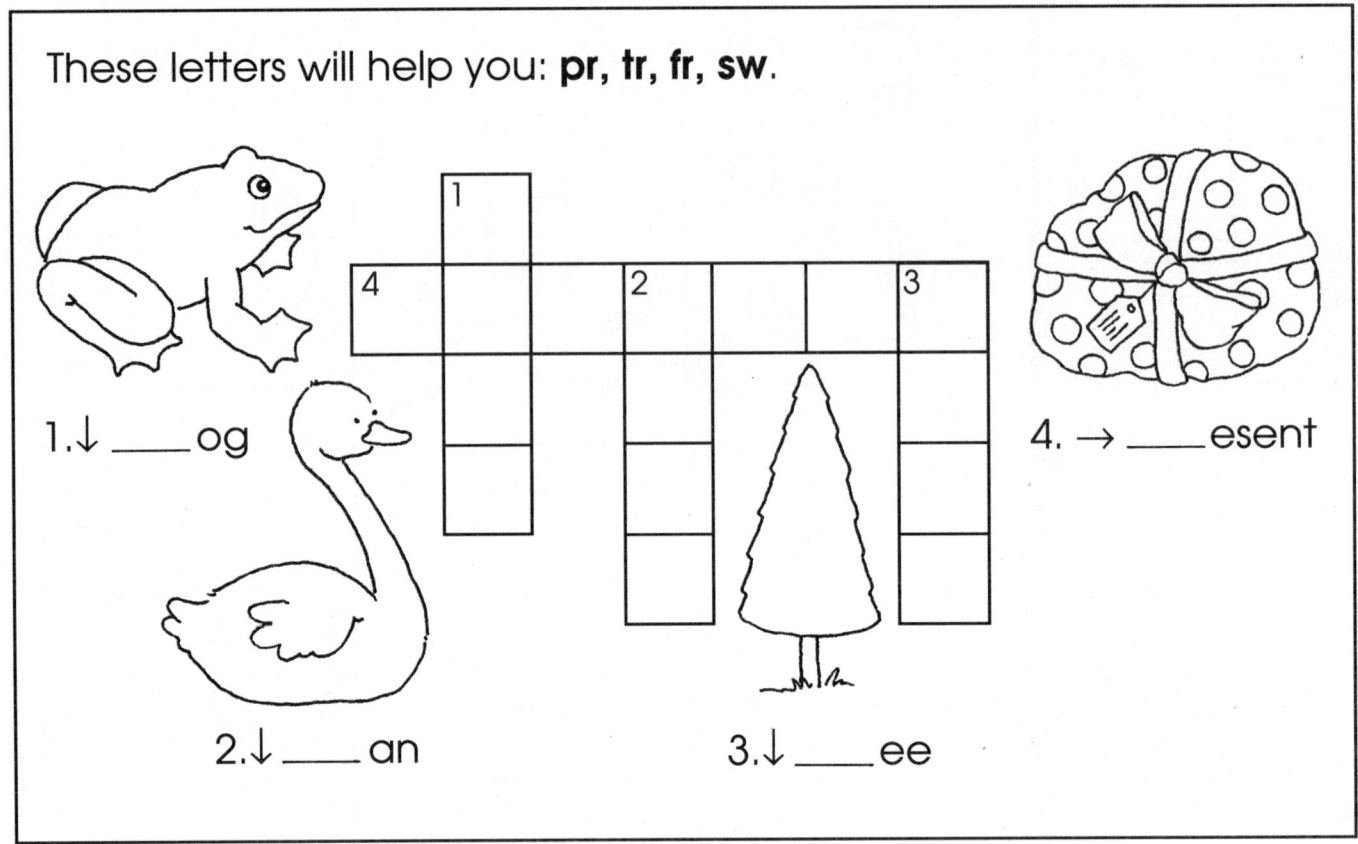

These letters will help you: **pr, tr, fr, sw**.

1.↓ ___og
2.↓ ___an
3.↓ ___ee
4.→ ___esent

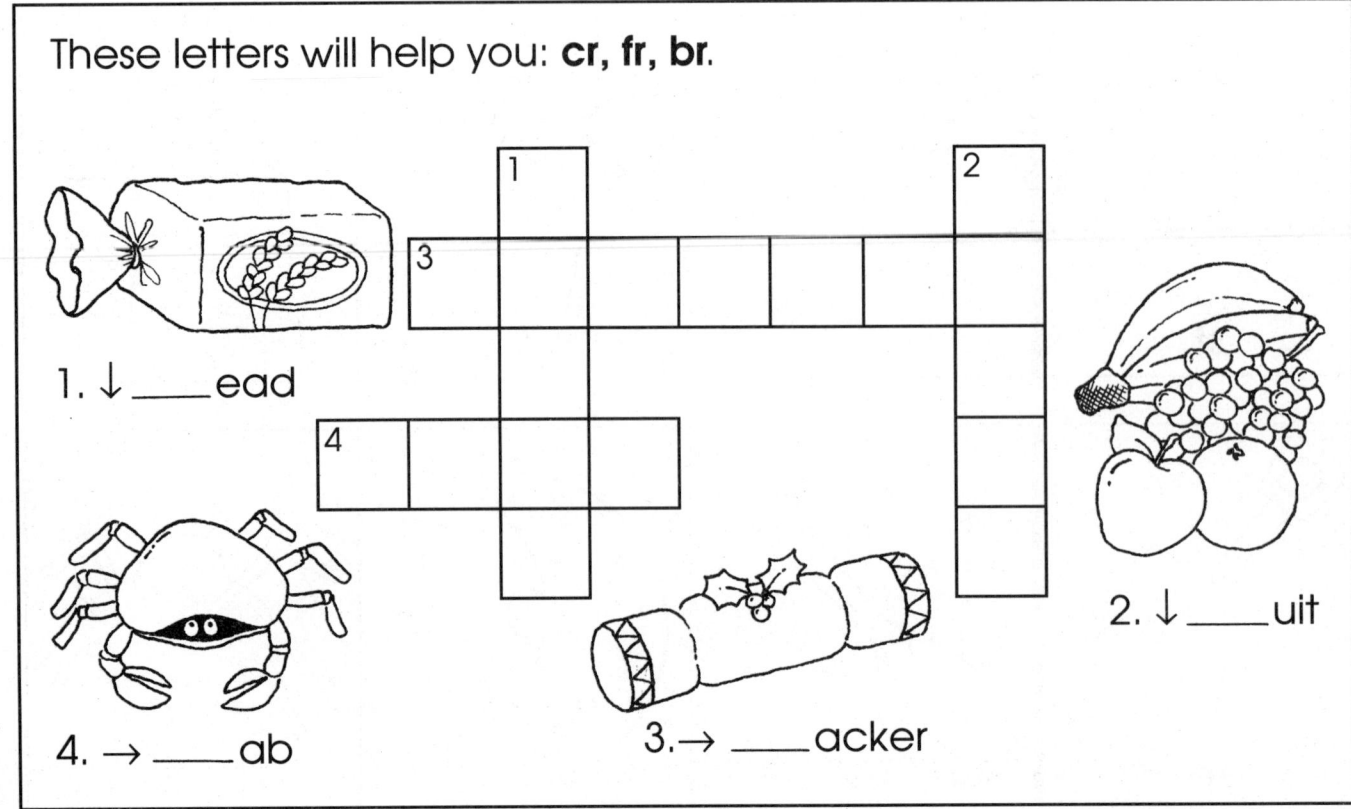

These letters will help you: **cr, fr, br**.

1.↓ ___ead
2.↓ ___uit
3.→ ___acker
4.→ ___ab

ESSENTIALS FOR ENGLISH: Rhymes and blends

Crosswords – 2

● Write in the missing letters, then fill in the crosswords.
These letters will help you: ch, sp, th, br.
These letters will help you: cl, gr, cr, dr.

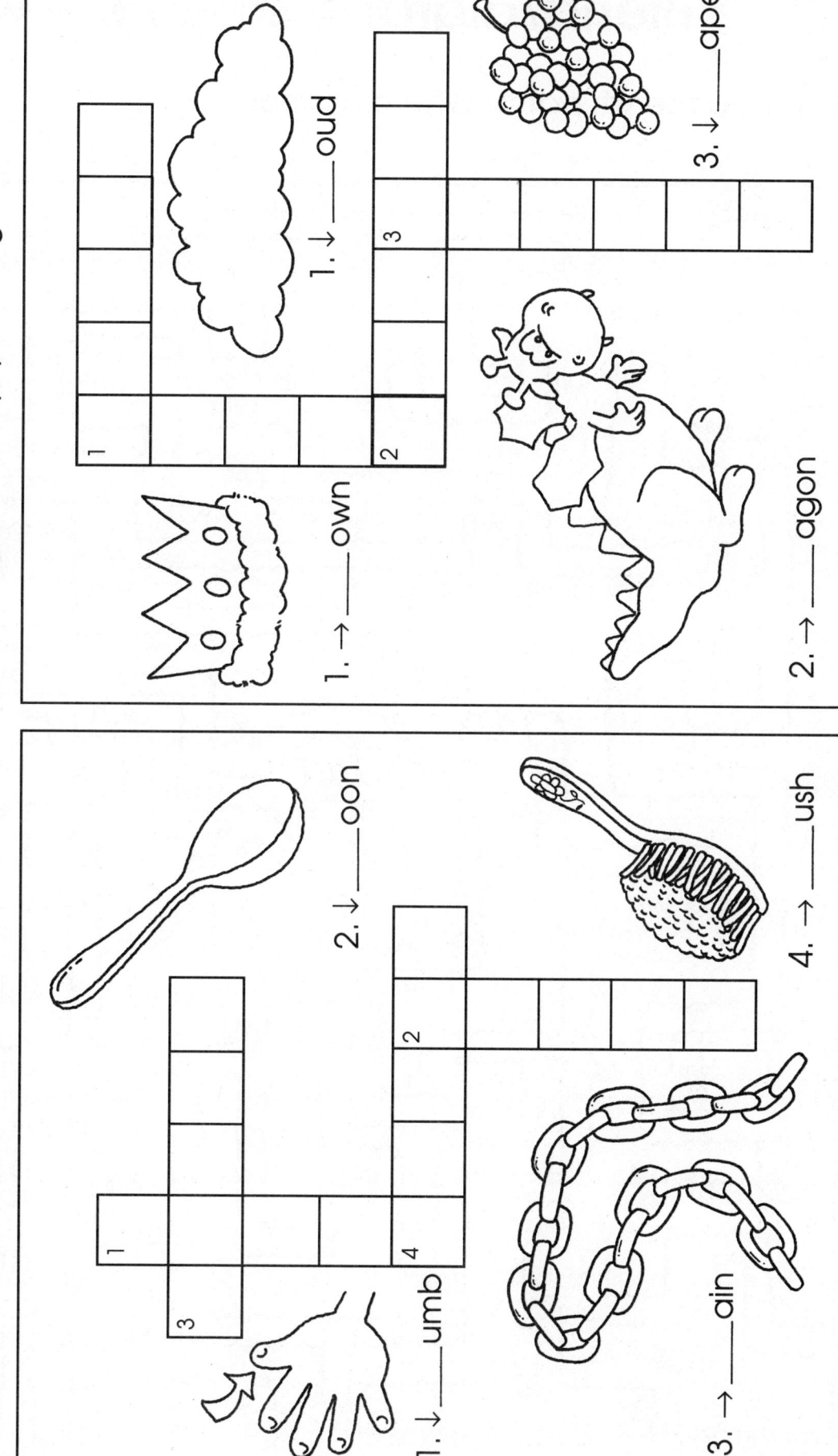

● Name _____

Blend/digraph sheet 6 – wh

● Follow the **wh** paths. Where do they take you?

ESSENTIALS FOR ENGLISH: Rhymes and blends

Digraph revision sheet
sh, ch and wh

- Look at the pictures. Can you find the following:
  - six things starting with **sh**;
  - four things starting with **ch**;
  - two things starting with **wh**.

- Write the letters on to the picture.

- **Name** _____

Word search – th

- Can you find the hidden words?

There are 12 different words starting with **th**.

t	h	e	l	h	m	t	h	i	n	k
e	p	t	h	a	n	k	s	y	r	h
t	h	e	r	e	b	t	h	o	s	e
b	l	k	d	l	h	t	h	i	s	b
r	k	t	h	e	y	t	h	e	s	e
t	h	e	i	r	n	u	j	i	b	o
b	t	h	i	n	g	h	t	h	i	n
t	h	a	t	l	u	r	g	p	e	i

- Write the words you have found in the space below.

_____ _____ _____

_____ _____ _____

_____ _____ _____

_____ _____ _____

Blend/digraph revision sheet – 1

● Some letters have fallen off the labels. Can you write them in?

● Which five toys would you like to buy? Write their names in the space below.

● Name _____

Blend/digraph revision sheet – 2

● Can you find something in the picture that begins with the following letters? **pl, ch, cl, dr, tr, fl, sh, st, gl, sc**

● Write the letters on to the picture.

ESSENTIALS FOR ENGLISH: Rhymes and blends

- Name _____

Blend/digraph revision sheet – 3

● Circle the correct starting letters under each picture.

cr br dr	sh sp cr	dr gr ch
fr br tr	gr sw cl	sm sn sw
ch sn th	pr br pl	th sh tr
sm st sn	bl pl cl	sl fl cl
tr fl sh	gl pr br	sh ch sl

ESSENTIALS FOR ENGLISH: Rhymes and blends

Name _____

Blend/digraph revision sheet – 4

● Circle the correct starting letters under each picture.

st sh sk	th st sh	th wh sh
pr dr br	sl st sp	cr dr sp
st sh sk	sc pr sw	gr sl wh
dr th sk	cr sw sn	pl sl cl
sc bl cr	tr gl ch	sh ch pr

● ESSENTIALS FOR ENGLISH: Rhymes and blends